D1280065

ALEXANDER MACKENZIE

Canadian Explorer

Also by Ronald Syme

BALBOA, FINDER OF THE PACIFIC
CAPTAIN COOK, PACIFIC EXPLORER
CARTIER, FINDER OF THE ST. LAWRENCE
CHAMPLAIN OF THE ST. LAWRENCE
COLUMBUS, FINDER OF THE NEW WORLD
CORTES OF MEXICO
DE SOTO, FINDER OF THE MISSISSIPPI
FIRST MAN TO CROSS AMERICA,
THE STORY OF CABEZA DEVACA
FRANCIS DRAKE, SAILOR OF THE UNKNOWN SEAS
FRANCISCO PIZARRO, FINDER OF PERU
HENRY HUDSON
JOHN SMITH OF VIRGINIA
LA SALLE OF THE MISSISSIPPI
MAGELLAN, FIRST AROUND THE WORLD
ON FOOT TO THE ARCTIC, THE STORY OF SAMUEL HEARNE
THE MAN WHO DISCOVERED THE AMAZON
VASCO DA GAMA, SAILOR TOWARD THE SUNRISE
WALTER RALEIGH
All illustrated by William Stobbs

BAY OF THE NORTH
Illustrated by Ralph Ray

AFRICAN TRAVELER, THE STORY OF MARY KINGSLEY
Illustrated by Jacqueline Tomes

ALEXANDER MACKENZIE

Canadian Explorer

BY RONALD SYME

Illustrated by William Stobbs

WILLIAM MORROW AND COMPANY

NEW YORK, 1964

Published simultaneously in the Dominion of
Canada by George J. McLeod Limited, Toronto

Printed in the United States of America

Library of Congress Catalog Card Number 64–10133

The long, slender birch-bark canoe came gliding onward across the surface of the lake. Touched here and there with strokes of bright ornamental paint, it stood out clearly against the gray surface of the water and equally gray Canadian sky. Not more than a mile ahead the gaunt outlines of a high wooden stockade were becoming visible on a low and rocky headland. It was the year 1788.

Jules Charbonnier, the dark-faced French

Canadian steersman, held up a hand to shield his eyes and gazed over the heads of the four paddlers. A distant speck that might have been a person was moving from the palisade toward the little wooden wharf, which projected into the water. Jules kept his sharp eyes fixed on the tiny figure for a while, and then uttered a brief grunt of satisfaction.

"Mr. Pond has already seen us," he announced, for the benefit of the young passenger who sat amidships. "He is advancing now to meet us."

Alexander Mackenzie, the passenger, raised a hand in a casual gesture to acknowledge the steersman's message. His own keen-sighted blue eyes, accustomed to gazing across a cold and wind-whipped sea, had also observed the tiny figure in the distance. But he had not mentioned the fact. A big-boned, rugged young Scotsman, Mackenzie was by nature as taciturn as any trapper in the Canadian wilds.

For more than two months now, the five canoemen had lived in the company of twenty-five-year-old Mackenzie. During that time they had traveled more than two thousand miles along the river and lake waterways that led across the American continent in a northwest direction from Montreal. Although Mackenzie remained a comparative stranger to his companions, he had surprised them by his remarkable handiness in the canoe. He was able to endure almost unlimited conditions of cold and wet and extreme discomfort. Whenever it became necessary to make a portage past an impassable rapids, Mackenzie was always ready to carry his fair share of burdens. During those two months, therefore, the *voyageurs* had come to respect Alexander Mackenzie as a natural leader, but they failed to understand his tough and silent nature.

Jules Charbonnier and his companions were

unaware that Mackenzie had been born in the tiny village of Stornoway on the island of Lewis, off the bitter northwest coast of Scotland. Poverty and hardship invariably made these islanders a frugal, self-reliant, and sturdy people. They had a reputation for being remarkably honest, hard-working, and—so it was said—a little too careful with money, or "too hard on the trigger," as Jules and his companions would have expressed it.

Mackenzie had all the traits of his fellow islanders, and they served him well. At the age of sixteen he emigrated from Scotland to the bustling, wealthy little frontier town of Montreal. There he found employment in a thriving firm of fur merchants. Since then he had worked his way up to partnership in the Northwest Fur Company.

This company was out to take business away from the old established, powerful but easygoing, Hudson's Bay Company. The North-

westers were hard, unscrupulous, ambitious, and venturesome. The senior partners had decided to send Mackenzie to take charge of their trading post at distant Fort Chipewyan on Lake Athabasca, which lies between the modern provinces of Alberta and Saskatchewan near their northern boundaries. Perhaps those partners found it prudent to have over-honest Mackenzie out of the way while they planned some of their peculiar business transactions. In any case, Peter Pond, the present manager of Fort Chipewyan, was fifty years old and would soon have to be relieved. After that age, life in those remote frontier trading posts became too hard. It was better to relieve such veterans while they were still fit and capable of performing their duties.

Pond released his steadying hold on the canoe as one of the *voyageurs* nimbly stepped ashore. He greeted Mackenzie with a brief nod, a curt word of welcome, and a powerful handshake. "You got here earlier than I expected," was all he said.

Later that same evening Mackenzie and Peter Pond sat in the manager's quarters at Fort Chipewyan. The frosty air inside the pine-log cabin made the fire burn brightly in the big stone hearth. The glow of the flames revealed two wooden sleeping bunks set against a wall, a row of leather-bound books on a hand-carved shelf, and a long-barreled musket and powder horn hanging from a wooden peg beside the door. The skins of bear and caribou covered the clumsy board floor. Outside the cabin, the dark and bitter cold of the late spring night hung heavy on the mist-veiled waters of the nearby lake.

The arrival of Mackenzie set Pond talking. In his harsh voice he gave the younger man some of his own vast knowledge of the immense territory. Lake Athabasca was as far west as any explorer had ever ventured. No one knew what lay farther in that same direction, other than that sooner or later there must be a west coast of the continent, washed by the warm waters of the Pacific Ocean.

"The Cree Indians who live round these parts," said Pond, "have a legend that some of the rivers run westward all the way to a great lake of salt water. They mean the sea, of course. Think of that, Mackenzie! No white man's ever got across Canada to the ocean. I used to hope I would make the trip but . . . well, it's too late for regrets now."

"There's a chain of high mountains along the western coast," said Mackenzie shrewdly. He was referring to the Rocky Mountains. "The Indians call them the Stony Mountains. How do you reckon the rivers run westward through them?"

"I've never figured that out," said old Pond obstinately. "But rivers find their way

through mountains most anywhere. I wanted to go there and see how they did it. And afterward I'd have gone down from those high, glittering peaks, all covered with untrodden snow, until I got a sight of the fine blue Pacific Ocean."

"If you ever had reached the coast," said Mackenzie, "you'd have tapped a great fur region. The Russians are there already. A British sea explorer called Captain Cook saw them there a few years ago. The Captain said that they were doing a fine trade in sea otter and Alaskan seal pelts. They ship the skins to Hong Kong, where they fetch a hundred and twenty dollars each. That's a fine profit; a very handsome profit indeed."

Old Pond thumped the arm of his chair. "I've heard about them furs on the coast," he said. "If we could find an overland route to the west, we could ship the bales back east just the way we're doing now. Soon settlers and fences and homesteads will be spreading into this territory, and we've got to find new fur-bearing territories before the Hudson's Bay Company does."

Pond was particularly bitter on the subject of the rival company. He said—and Mackenzie agreed with him—that for the past hundred years its traders had been sitting behind the palisades of their forts waiting for the Indians to bring them furs. Such men

were, Pond added contemptuously, a poor-spirited lot. They were afraid of their rich and greedy masters in London, afraid of the Indians, afraid of the winter weather. Most of all they were afraid of losing their way in the wilderness. But conditions were changing nowadays. Trade rivalry was forcing the Hudson's Bay Company to become more daring. They were starting to follow the risky example set by the Northwest Company, going out to meet the Indians in their own tribal territories. This bitter and increasing rivalry was already making both companies desperately eager to stake a claim to rich, new fur-bearing regions.

Mackenzie, the cool-headed astute Scotsman, was as absorbed in this search as anyone else. Now as he leaned forward to stir the fire into a blaze—the midnight cold was beginning to seep into the cabin—he asked another question.

"What river would you have followed, Pond, if you'd ever set out to reach the Pacific Ocean?"

Loneliness and isolation had made Pond naturally distrustful of human nature. Although the two clerks attached to Fort Chipewyan were asleep in their own log cabin on the other side of the compound, and the canoemen were busy celebrating with the Indian hunters in their own quarters, it took the veteran a long time to give his answer. He spoke almost in a gruff whisper, as if he were afraid of being overheard.

"There are two likely rivers," he said. Then he went on to describe them. One was called the Unjigah, or Peace River, by the local Indians, and flowed into the western end of Lake Athabasca, not far from Fort Chipewyan. The second river flowed out of the western end of Slave Lake, which lay some two hundred miles to the north of Fort Chipewyan. Pond himself had gone there by canoe only two years before to examine the stream. It was an imposingly large river and it certainly seemed to follow a westerly course.

"What's important about it," said Pond, "is that some Indian hunters I met up in that territory told me the river flowed into salt water after making a great long journey across the land. If what they say is right, the salt water might be the Pacific Ocean.

It's the Slave River I'd try for a start. In fact, I was planning to do it when I heard the Company was going to take me out of here."

Peter Pond left with the *voyageurs* when they began their return journey to far-off Montreal. Alexander Mackenzie was now in full charge of Fort Chipewyan. In a leather-bound diary he had already carefully noted down everything that the old fur trader had told him. Those two unexplored and mysterious rivers were beginning to interest him greatly. He was eager to carry on exploration from the point where old Pond had been forced to leave off.

Like so many of the Highland Scots, Mackenzie had a great love of culture. It was not surprising, therefore, that he soon became tired of the dreary little trading post beside the islet-studded waters of Lake Athabasca and the low gray hills that surrounded it.

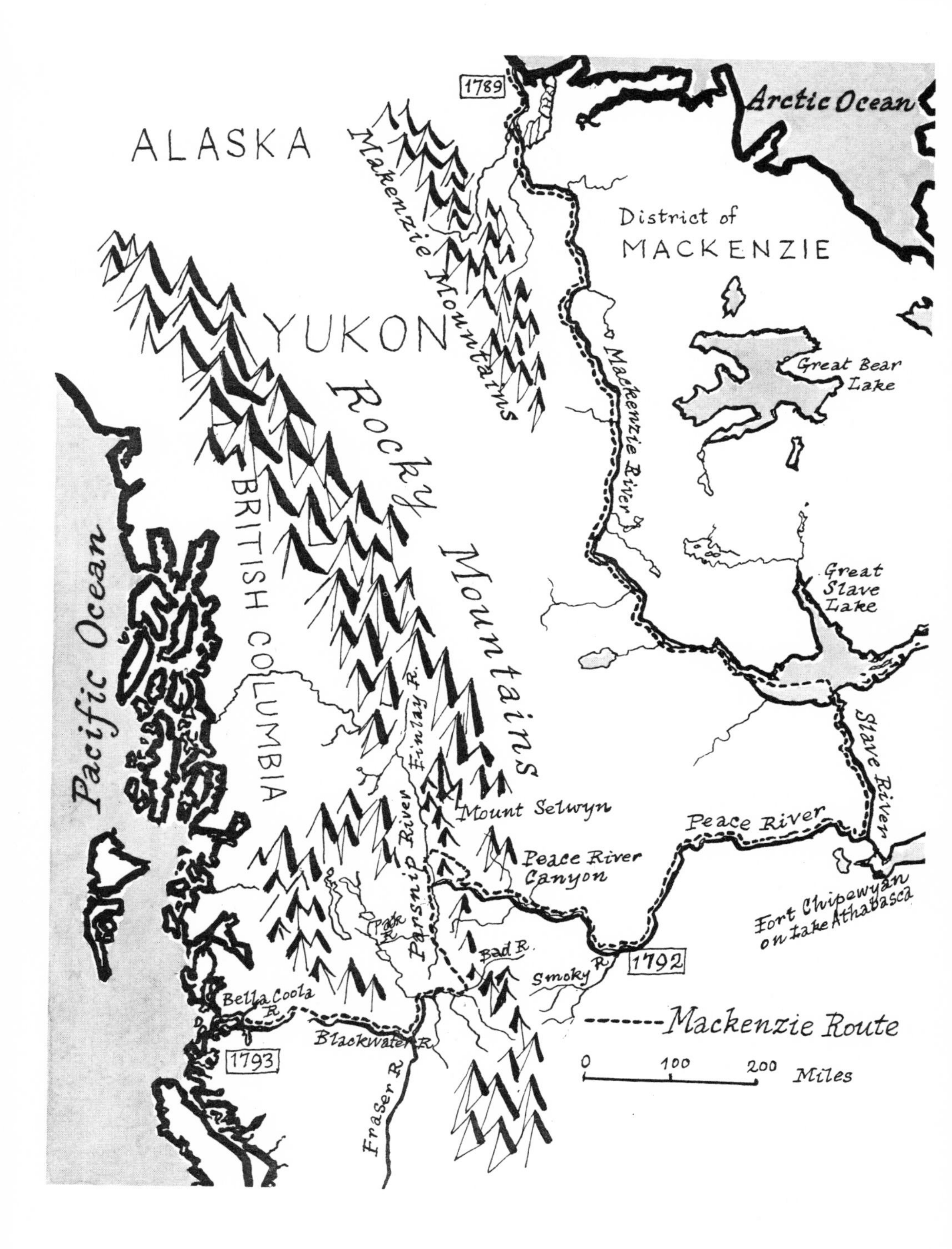
1789
Arctic Ocean
ALASKA
Makenzie Mountains
District of
MACKENZIE
YUKON
Mackenzie River
Great Bear Lake
Rocky
Mountains
BRITISH COLUMBIA
Pacific Ocean
Great Slave Lake
Finlay R.
Slave River
Mount Selwyn
Peace River
Parsnip River
Peace River Canyon
Pack R.
Fort Chipewyan on Lake Athabasca
Bad R.
1792
Smoky R.
Bella Coola R.
Mackenzie Route
Blackwater R.
1793
0
100
200
Miles
Fraser R.

The monotonous existence at the fort was unable to hold either his interest or imagination.

By April, 1789, Mackenzie's curiosity about the unknown rivers became overwhelming.

"Dear Rory," he wrote to his cousin Roderick in Montreal, "if you could come up here for the summer, I'd be grateful. There's a trip I'm thinking of making, and the post will need someone in charge while I'm gone."

Roderick was another successful young partner in the Northwest Company and more or less free to please himself. The summer was a slack time in the fur trade. There would be little for him to do at Fort Chipewyan while Alexander Mackenzie was absent. Roderick came at once, traveling by the great system of waterways that stretched almost all the way from Montreal to Lake Athabasca. By the time he reached the fort, his cousin's first voyage of exploration was about to begin.

Beside the wooden landing stage floated two canoes. Alexander Mackenzie intended to paddle upstream in them to Great Slave Lake and thence along the river, which, according to Pond, flowed westward out of it.

The large canoe was thirty-two feet long, five feet wide amidships, narrowing at both ends to two feet six inches. It was built of fine yellow birch bark, stretched over seventy-one ribs of thin white cedar. The up-curved bow and stern were gaudily painted with a strange Indian design. Along the bottom of the canoe lay a platform of three-inch poles on which rested twenty-five bales of goods, each weighing ninety pounds. Apart from this ton of cargo, the big canoe was to carry Mackenzie himself, four French Canadian *voyageurs*, two of their Indian wives, and a young man named John Steinbruck. He was a German visitor to Canada, who had accompanied Rory Mackenzie up to Athabasca by way of

having a great adventure. When fully loaded, the big canoe's gunwales were within six inches of the water.

"When Steinbruck first saw her," Roderick told his cousin with a chuckle, "he said he wouldn't agree to sail round the shores of the lake in her! I've assured him the boat is quite usual."

The second and smaller canoe, which was much less elaborate, held an Indian leader graced by the nickname of English Chief. He was a gaunt, silent man, very proud of his English nickname and extremely hard on his own people. With him were two of his wives. "The best I've got for a journey like this," he explained to Mackenzie. There were also three young Indian braves, who would act as hunters for the whole party. Mackenzie, the careful Scotsman, was carrying a great load of provisions, but he preferred to save expenses by living off wild game wherever possible.

Voyageurs were known to be the best canoemen in Canada. Mackenzie's were short, sturdy fellows, picturesque in brightly colored stocking caps, embroidered woolen jackets, and tasseled deerskin knee pants. Their physical strength was enormous. They could carry with ease a ninety-pound burden on their backs, and sometimes, to earn an extra dollar or two, they carried double that load for miles. Their favorite diet was fish—though they would eat anything else to satisfy their vast appetites—and their favorite drink was rum. They lived and played hard, counted themselves lucky if they earned $150 a year in return for working like slaves, and were old men before they were forty. Without these hard, experienced canoemen, explorers such as Mackenzie could never have made their great journeys.

Up the Slave River went the canoes. The wide stream flowed between low-lying banks covered with spruce, poplar, birch, tamarack, and willow.

By the eighteenth of June, Mackenzie had reached the river that flowed westward out of Great Slave Lake. Driving his party with untiring energy, he began to follow it. Always by four o'clock in the chill pre-dawn hours, the little flotilla was ready for the day's journey. Not until seven o'clock in the evening would the men make camp again. The hunters shot game as the canoes paddled along, and the whole party fed well on caribou, swans, geese, hares, and partridges.

Five hundred miles up that river, Mackenzie began to grow worried. He was continually taking compass bearings and results showed him that they were traveling northward. The river, after swinging to the west as Pond had said, was now following a course that could lead only to the Arctic Ocean instead of the Pacific Ocean.

Early in July they reached a rocky, desolate country, where ice lingered in shady pools and a bitter wind swept down from the surrounding hills at night. This was the country of the Slave Indians. When Mackenzie spoke to them through English Chief, they were far from encouraging.

"Only rocks and ice and pitiless cold await you farther north," one of them said. "If

you don't die of hunger, the Eskimos will certainly kill you. There is also a spirit in the river, which swallows many travelers in canoes."

But Mackenzie kept pushing northward. He had to be sure that this river did not turn westward again. Even the decreasing supply of game and the reluctance of the Slave Indian guides he hired could not make him give up the journey. Every night the temperature dropped lower and lower. The *voyageurs* and Indians, tough people though they were, huddled more closely around the evening fires blazing in their tents. By the fourteenth of July the whole ugly countryside was so bare and desolate that even the trained Indian hunters could find no game. Those hungry fourteen people, men and women, began to devour with enormous appetites the untouched provisions they had brought from Fort Chipewyan.

Mackenzie noted in his diary for July 15:

> I told them that I intended to keep going northward for another seven days. If I did not get to the sea, I would return. The low state of the provisions . . . ensured that I would honor this agreement.

On the seventeenth of July, 1789, forty days after they had left Fort Chipewyan, Mackenzie camped on an island in midstream. His calculations showed that they had reached sixty-nine degrees north latitude. This meant that they were well into the Arctic Circle. Mackenzie had given up all hope of the river's ever turning westward. Having come so far, he was now merely curious to see where it entered the Arctic Ocean. At least this would be new knowledge. He wrote in his diary:

> As soon as the tents were pitched, I or-

dered the nets to be set, and I went with English Chief to the highest part of the island. We discovered solid ice extending from the southwest by compass to the eastward.

During that night Mackenzie was awakened from his usual light sleep by loud shouting from the canoemen's tents. "The river," they yelled, "is rising. We've got to get the baggage onto higher ground."

For a moment Mackenzie was puzzled. Then he guessed the reason for what was happening. This was no flood. They had reached the ocean and the tide was coming in. His *voyageurs*, having lived far from the sea all their lives, were not accustomed to the rise and fall of the tides. Although the water in the river was still fresh, it was being affected by the nearby Arctic Ocean.

The weather cleared next morning, and

Mackenzie saw in the distance a stretch of bright blue ocean, covered with gleaming ice-bergs. Large white porpoises were playing in the freezing water, but they were the only sign of life in this desolate territory.

This was the bitter end of twenty-six-year-old Mackenzie's first journey of exploration. Instead of reaching the Pacific coast, he and his thirteen companions were gazing at the Arctic Ocean.

They began the return journey with as little delay as possible. Mackenzie was faced with the alarming fact that the canoes carried only enough food to last another seven days. But the short arctic summer was bringing game northward. The hunters' muskets were banging loudly soon after they left the arc-tic shore behind. Eight days later, Mackenzie wrote:

We have not touched any of our pro-

vision stores for six days, in which time we have consumed two reindeer, four swans, forty-five geese, and a considerable quantity of fish. I have always observed that the north men possessed very hearty appetites.

The supplies of food were more plentiful during that homeward voyage, but conditions otherwise were worse. The canoemen were

growing tired from the constant portages past bad sections of the river, where they had to carry the canoes for considerable distances and every one of those ninety-pound packages as well. The current was against them all the way, and at times it reached a velocity of eight or nine miles an hour. Paddling became useless, and even poling the canoes upstream was often impossible. On those occasions the men had to start "tracking," which meant going ashore with a towline and trudging along the bank, hauling the canoe behind them. One day they would journey under a hot sun, constantly being bitten by clouds of ever-hungry mosquitoes. The next day they would shiver with cold as they stumbled over sharp-pointed rocks with feet half-numbed by the icy water.

There were other misfortunes as well. English Chief and the hunters were becoming resentful of the discipline of the march and the speed with which Mackenzie—a careful but relentless leader—drove the expedition along day after day. They threatened desertion. Mackenzie had to coax them back into good humor with a gift of powerful rum. Then, when they came to Great Slave Lake, the water was so rough that it almost swamped the canoes. For a while Mackenzie and his followers faced death by drowning.

The big canoe lost one of its sails in this

storm, and the smaller canoe containing English Chief, his two wives, and the three hunters was wrecked. "This evening," noted Mackenzie, "I gave my men some rum to cheer them after their fatigues."

But not even rum could now persuade English Chief to go any farther. He had had enough of cold and misery and never-ending labor. At his own wish he was left behind with his wives and the hunters, comfortably installed in a tent beside a small lake filled with fish and in a countryside swarming with deer and game.

"From now on my people and I will travel at our own rate," English Chief told Mackenzie. "We should reach Fort Chipewyan in about two months' time."

On the twenty-second of September, when the skies overhead were filled with swans, cranes, geese, and ducks speeding southward to avoid the approaching winter, Mackenzie's

canoes came down the last stretch of the river and sailed across Lake Athabasca to the headland where Fort Chipewyan stood.

Mackenzie was as economical with words as he was with everything else. The account he wrote of his great northward trip was a model of concise language. He ended it with the unassuming sentence: ". . . we concluded this journey which had occupied the considerable space of one hundred and two days."

As far as Mackenzie was concerned, the 3000-mile journey he had made was a mere waste of time, for he had failed to reach the Pacific Ocean. He took no credit for the fact that his journey finally proved to geographers that their old dream of a seaway between the Atlantic and the Pacific, lying somewhere in the Far North, was completely inaccurate. Mackenzie named the great river he had explored Disappointment. Little did he dream that one day it would be renamed after him and become the Mackenzie River, the second longest river on the continent.

The senior partners of the Northwest Fur Company were interested in little except the yearly profits they made. They were hard and narrow-minded men with few ideas about anything except their cashboxes. When Mackenzie saw them in Montreal and reported on his journey, these fellow Scots listened with bored inattention. They failed to realize the outstanding importance of the Mackenzie River Basin as a great fur territory. They merely wanted to know how many bales of skins had been obtained from the Indians at Fort Chipewyan, and how many gallons of rum and pounds of tobacco, gunpowder, and lead had been traded in exchange.

"My expedition was hardly spoken of," Mackenzie wrote to Roderick from Montreal, "but that is what I expected."

During the next two years, from 1789 to 1791, Mackenzie worked hard at Fort Chipewyan to make this outpost the most flourishing one owned by the Northwest Company. Using the knowledge he had gained, he rapidly extended trade in the Mackenzie Basin (its later name) to Indians who were eager to barter their furs in exchange for brass kettles and sheet iron, lengths of linen, and flints for their muskets.

Mackenzie succeeded in his ambition. Now he was able to take the next step in his carefully thought-out plans. In the fall of 1791 he welcomed back to Fort Chipewyan his stolid and faithful cousin Roderick from Montreal. Once again Roderick had agreed to take charge of the outpost.

"That trip I made to the Arctic Ocean taught me a lot of things," said Mackenzie. "One of them was that I know too little about astronomy and navigation and geography. A tutor would be better than all the scientific books I've been studying alone. I'm off to London to get myself taught more thoroughly."

"It will take you quite a while, no doubt," the placid Roderick replied. "No matter. I'll stay here gladly until you come back."

Mackenzie spent the winter of 1791 and 1792 in London, England. Living in cheap lodgings, which seemed luxurious by comparison with the austere quarters at Fort Chipe-

wyan, he trudged daily along the crowded and muddy streets to his tutor's house. This teacher was a crusty old Naval officer on half pay, who was a brilliant expert in the subjects he taught. Mackenzie spent his spare time and a good deal of his money in selecting more scientific books and the finest navigational instruments. All the time he read and memorized and studied. Gradually he brought himself up-to-date with what was happening on the Pacific coast of America.

Spain was at last making half-hearted attempts to occupy that whole territory. The absence of wealthy Indian tribes to loot and the arid desert lying across the north of Mexico had hitherto discouraged her pioneers. Now they were starting to push northward. Already they had founded a settlement at San Diego. At Monterey and San Francisco mud forts had been built and garrisoned with Spanish soldiery. Meanwhile, Russian fur traders were advancing rapidly across the Aleutian Islands. Spain had already suggested to the Empress of Russia that Prince William Sound in Alaska should be the boundary between Russian and Spanish America. The coast to the south of that was to remain a Spanish possession. Unless Canada and America could be persuaded to take an early interest, the whole seaboard might become foreign territory. Both countries would thus be cut off from access to the Pacific Ocean.

But if English-speaking colonists could settle on the coast, thought Mackenzie, it would give their countries a greater claim on the whole region. The way to bring that about is to prove to our own fur traders, pioneers, and colonists that one can reach the Pacific coast by an overland route. They'll go there gladly when they know it can be done.

Past lakes stocked with whitefish, across

swamps where wild rice flourished, along rivers on whose banks grew unspoiled groves of oak and maple, birch and pine, Mackenzie traveled the long road westward back to Fort Chipewyan. He arrived in October, 1792.

"I mean to explore the Peace River," he told Roderick. "Pond was wrong—as he thought he might be—about the Slave River; he may be right about the Peace. Possibly the way to the west that I am looking for lies somewhere beyond its source."

Mackenzie was in a great hurry to start his second journey. He decided to spend the winter in camp just above the junction of the Smoky and Peace Rivers, a spot which lay two hundred and fifty miles west of Chipewyan. When spring came he would have that much distance less to travel.

Those winter months passed slowly in that wilderness of snow and dark pine forests. With Mackenzie were Joseph Landry and Charles

Ducette, two *voyageurs* who had been with him on his trip to the Arctic Ocean. There were also four other French Canadian canoemen, skilled and hardy fellows who had agreed to make the journey. They were François Beaulieux, Baptist Bisson, François Courtois, and Jacques Beauchamp. Two Cree Indians had been chosen as hunters, and Mackenzie had picked a fellow Scotsman named Alexander Mackay as his second-in-command. Mackay was a clerk in the Northwest Company. He was a big, powerful man, more suited to roughing it in the wilds than sitting on a stool in a dusty office. Somewhere or other Mackenzie had also acquired a dog. He was a big animal, mostly Indian mongrel, but with a dash of Irish wolfhound and English sheep dog. He may not have been handsome, but he was highly intelligent, and Mackenzie was very fond of him.

They were ready to set off on the ninth of

May, 1793. During the winter the canoemen had made a big canoe of which Mackenzie was extremely proud.

Her dimensions were twenty-five feet long within, exclusive of the curves of stem and stern, twenty-six inches high, and four feet nine inches across. At the same time she was so light that two men could carry her on a good road three or four miles without resting. In this slender vessel, we shipped provisions, goods for presents, arms, ammunition, and baggage to the weight of three thousand pounds, and an equipage of ten people.

Mackenzie was soon disappointed with his canoe. The craft would have been handy on the deep and tranquil waters of a lake, but it was no match for the wild Peace River. At the end of the first day's journey upstream, Mackenzie wrote: "The canoe, being strained from its having been very heavily laden, became so leaky that we were obliged to land, unload, and gum it."

From then on, the varying condition of that canoe became a matter of almost daily concern to Mackenzie. The river tugged at it, pierced and broke it on underwater boulders, strained it unbearably in foaming rapids. As its birch-bark hull and light cedar timbers slowly became waterlogged, it grew heavier. The canoemen came to hate their craft as they struggled to portage it up steep slopes and along forest paths. No one but men of their patient and enduring strength and experience would have been willing to go on coping with that sagging, leaky, and abominably heavy canoe. Other men would have chopped it up for firewood, or hurled it into the river in disgust. But the success or failure of Mackenzie's journey depended on the canoe, therefore he had to cherish it, like a poor invalid, for a long time yet.

For the next eight days they fought their way upstream against the swiftening current of the Peace River. The stream widened gradually to eight hundred yards and was full of little islets and sandbanks. Whenever they landed, they saw the tracks of many grizzly bears. Once they actually came across a den where one of these huge animals had hiber-

nated. It measured ten feet long, five feet high, and six feet wide. The two Indian hunters with Mackenzie peered into this den fearfully. Mackenzie noted:

> The Indians [are greatly afraid] of this kind of bear, which is called the grizzly bear, and they never venture to attack it but in a party of at least three or four.

Two nights later Mackenzie sat beside the campfire and wrote in his diary:

> The Rocky Mountains appeared in sight, with their summits covered with snow, bearing southwest by south. They formed a very agreeable object to every person in the canoe, as we [saw] them much sooner than we expected.

But as the Peace River drew nearer to the

mountains, its nature began to change. Mackenzie did not know it, but they were approaching the twenty-five-mile-long Peace River Canyon. In bygone ages the water had carved out a narrow passage for itself through the mountains. This channel was no more than fifty yards wide, and the river, which in more level country sometimes attained a comfortable width of over a mile, rushed through it, swirling and impatient, with an angry thunder. Almost sheer walls of stone rose on each side of this deadly canyon to a height of ten or eleven hundred feet. The gravel banks and rocky shelves at the bottom of these great walls trembled constantly under the giant pressure of the green, bitterly cold, and terrifying mass of water.

The river was already in flood and still rising, but Mackenzie did not know this either. He and his party began to fight their way up-stream through the canyon. Sometimes they poled, sometimes they portaged their canoe, but usually they tracked it by stumbling and splashing along the narrow and dangerous banks, hauling the towline.

> We continued our course for about three quarters of a mile. We could now proceed no further on this side of the water, and [crossing to the other side] was rendered extremely dangerous, not only

from the strength of the current, but by the cascades just below us, which, if we had got amongst them, would have involved us and the canoe in one common destruction. . . . The current on the west side was almost equally violent . . . but we were enabled to tow the canoe till we came to the foot of the most rapid cascade we had hitherto seen. Here we unloaded, and carried everything over a rocky point. When the canoe was reloaded . . . one false step of those who were attached to the line, or the breaking of the line itself, would have at once consigned the canoe and everything in it to instant destruction.

That overstrained rope did actually break when a sudden vicious wave slapped against the canoe. The vessel staggered for a moment and then began to charge downstream, with three unfortunate men still aboard it.

Only death awaited them in the rapids below, but a sudden miracle occurred. Another wave, appearing from nowhere, again struck the canoe and brought it swinging in close to the bank. One of the canoemen jumped for his life, landed in shallow water, and braced his feet against the rocks. He managed to hold the canoe until his two companions and the men who had been towing were able to come to his assistance. This shock-

ingly narrow escape almost broke the courage of the Canadian *voyageurs*, but by the following morning they had forgotten last night's grumbles and fears and were ready to go forward again.

Mackenzie had entered the canyon on the eighteenth of May. Five days later—the morning after the canoe broke adrift—they gave up trying to fight against the river. The Indian hunters, who had gone exploring ahead on foot, reported that nine miles farther on the river again became navigable.

"We'll cut through the forest," said Mackenzie, "and carry the canoe the rest of the way."

They actually made that incredible journey, and the long-suffering canoe survived the trip. Mackenzie reckoned the actual distance they covered was seven miles, but to the unfortunate men carrying their monstrous burdens over mountaintops and through snow-filled defiles it probably seemed at least double that distance. In this manner they succeeded in climbing into the midst of the snow-covered Rockies. On Friday, May 25, 1793, they were in the hills above the Peace River Canyon.

In later years it was sometimes said that Alexander Mackenzie verged on being a slave driver in the way he urged his men forward. The story is told that when his second-in-

command, big, patient Alexander Mackay, developed frostbite in his toes while in the Rockies, Mackenzie became unreasonably angry with him. "After all," he is reported to have said, "there was scarce thirty degrees of frost last night and you had a whole blanket to sleep under. You must have been careless, Alex, just downright careless!"

Whatever the truth about tough, bearded, blue-eyed Mackenzie, a descendant of the oldtime Vikings, the fact remains that his men, however much they grumbled, continued to follow him. There were occasions when they could have deserted him without saying a word, or else refused to go forward another step. They may not have liked him, but his fearlessness, courage, and willingness to take his daily share in the toil earned their deep respect.

But after conquering the Peace River and reaching the heights of the Rockies, those sturdy fellows with Mackenzie must have winced when he began to grumble at the slow progress they were making! "It's almost the end of May," he told them. "We've been on the road for nineteen days, but we've covered only two hundred and fifty miles. Yonder lie more ranges of the mountains we've got to cross. It'll be sadly late in the season before we step down to the coast. We've got to travel faster."

They went forward once again, the canoe still accompanying them over the granite mountains. A day or two later they were passing the glittering peak of Mount Selwyn, which rose to a height of 6220 feet. Mackenzie wrote:

> An extensive view opened upon us displaying a beautiful sheet of water. Here the wooded mountains opened on either

side, so that we entertained the hope of soon leaving them behind.

Mackenzie was too optimistic about those mountains. Before they reached the coast he would have to find a path through yet another range. The truth is that he was becoming desperately weary of mountains of every kind, of cold and treacherous rivers, of endless groping for an unknown route, and of the almost constant grumbling and reluctance of his *voyageurs* to go any farther into the unknown. It has sometimes been said that Mackenzie had no appreciation of the splendid scenery he came across. He was probably too tired and had so much on his mind that he was in no mood to admire the majesty of the great mountains. His one desire, as he himself said, was to "leave them behind."

On the last day of May, Mackenzie reached a deep valley with pine-clad sides where two rivers came together, one from the north, the other from the south. The stream that flowed down from the north (later known as the Finlay) was broad and deep and smooth. The river from the south (later known as the Parsnip) was swifter flowing and much narrower, an ugly stream for any canoe to tackle.

Mackenzie remembered the words of an old Indian warrior they had met earlier on the journey. "You will come to a spot where two rivers meet," the Indian had told him. "You will be tempted to take the one which flows down from the north, for it is a handsome river. Do not fall into the trap it makes for unwary travelers. It wanders away into the mountains and there it loses itself in little streams. You must take the southern river. Like a true friend, it will not betray you. Go in your canoe up this river. After three or four days, you will come to the mouth of a little stream. You will know the place by the black embers of campfires where traveling Indian parties have encamped. There will be other signs of Indians as well. You must go ashore at this point. Camp beside the little stream overnight if you wish; there is plenty of game to be found in the nearby woods. Next day you must portage south. By the evening you will come to another larger river, which will carry you safely and easily toward the midday sun."

From experience in the past, Mackenzie knew how unreliable advice given by Indians could be. Very often they made up some fanciful story to conceal their ignorance. Sometimes they gave the questioner the answer they imagined he wished to have. This Indian, however, gave the impression of being sincere and his words had remained in Mackenzie's mind. Now, as they stood gazing down at the two rivers so different in nature, he decided to trust the Indian's advice.

"We'll take the southern stream," he said.

The *voyageurs* almost mutinied on the spot. "Why paddle up a wild mountain river in flood," one demanded, "when before us lies another wider and peaceful river, where a canoe can be paddled along with comfort?"

"Because the southern river is the right one," said Mackenzie, and there the matter ended. Grumbling among themselves, their dark faces grim with disapproval, the *voyageurs* launched their rickety canoe on the wild waters of the Parsnip.

During the next three days Mackenzie often wondered if he had done wisely to follow the old Indian's advice. The river was proving almost as bad as the Peace River Canyon. The gravelly shores were submerged by the flooding water so it was impossible to tow the canoe upstream. Poling and paddling were useless against the fast current. The only way they could travel was by pulling the canoe

along by holding onto the branches of the trees that bordered the river.

During the exhausting voyage, Mackenzie made one of his few mistakes. He had been going short of sleep for a whole month and was beginning to feel the effects of it. "I was in the habit of sometimes indulging myself with a short doze in the canoe," he wrote.

He was asleep when they came to the mouth

of the stream where they should have disembarked and portaged overland. Mackenzie must have forgotten to warn Mackay and the others to look out for the place, and by the time he woke up they were well past the Indian camping ground without his being aware of it.

Having missed this river (the Pack it was called later) they went on up the Parsnip River. The water became shallower and the gray, granite banks drew closer together. At last they reached a dismal area where little mountain streams wandered in all directions. The countryside was a mass of shallow lakes. Trees grew out of the water and millions of beaver dams utterly blocked all further progress. It was raining heavily that day. Cold, tired, and utterly discouraged, the *voyageurs* collected wild parsnips and cooked them with pemmican, dried meat packed in grease and stored in leather bags. Then they lay down to sleep in the rain, around a smoldering, half-hearted fire.

This time Mackenzie was really almost beaten. "Our only hope," he said later, "was in such information as we should be able to procure from the natives."

It was very unlikely, however, that even the poorest Indians would choose to inhabit such a wet, dreary, miserable district. And yet that very miracle occurred. Next day, on the ninth of June, they actually met some Indians.

It was Joseph Landry, the veteran *voyageur*, who suddenly announced, "I smell smoke. There is a fire burning near here."

Mackenzie went forward to investigate. He walked along several beaver dams until he reached a patch of higher ground, which was screened from sight by young spruce trees. There stood an Indian tent and beside it blazed a cooking fire. He was sighted immediately. Two Indian warriors came rushing toward him with leveled spears, while the women around the fire uttered loud cries of terror.

Mackenzie came to a standstill and raised one hand above his head in the usual sign of peace. Gradually the charging Indians slowed down. Seeing that Mackenzie was unarmed, they dropped their spears and drew tomahawks from their belts. They approached him in a cautious circling manner.

"Peace," said Mackenzie, using one of the few Indian words he knew. "Friend, friend."

One of his Indian hunters appeared at that moment, hastening to see what had happened to his leader. This man called loudly to the two warriors, who were peering suspiciously at Mackenzie.

"What sort of man is this?" one of the warriors shouted back. "His skin is white, and he has frightened our women."

"He is a white man," the interpreter called. "He comes from beyond the mountains. He will give you presents if you befriend him. There are nine of us with him. Lay aside your axes, friends."

Mackenzie's quick eyes had already noticed that the tomahawks the Indians held were fitted with iron heads. This meant that they must be in touch with Europeans who had come to the west coast by sea.

The two parties gradually made friends. There were three Indian warriors, three women, and seven or eight children. None of them had ever seen a European before. As their fear left them, they began to talk more freely.

"We get the iron from another tribe who live farther to the west," one of them explained. "They travel for one moon to a country where an Indian tribe live in fine houses and trade their skins and furs for this iron

and other useful things as well. Men come in great canoes (ships) and bring these things across the Stinking Lake (sea)."

These Indians Mackenzie had met proved very useful. One of them agreed to act as guide. Like his friends, he was a man of middle height, with a round face, long hair, and high cheekbones. He wore the usual costume of moccasins, leggings, which reached to the hip, and a kind of jacket made either of beaver skins or caribou hide. Both the men and women of his party wore across the face, under the eyes, a painted black stripe, which reached from ear to ear.

Indians and white men camped together in friendly manner that night. Next morning Mackenzie's new guide explained the route they would take. "Near this river where we are now," he said, "there are three small lakes. We pass along them and then we come to a larger river that flows toward the noon-

day sun. If we travel down it we will come to the Stinking Lake."

At sunset on June 12, Mackenzie and his men stood gazing down at yet another rocky, fast-flowing, and dangerous river. Behind them lay the rugged upland region and the three little lakes. The air seemed warmer that evening, and the trees had a softer, kindlier appearance.

For the moment, however, Mackenzie was

not interested in the changing appearance of the countryside. The compass he held in his hand was indicating the delightful fact that this river flowed *westward*. He knew then that they were over the great mountains that separated the American plains and forests from the Pacific coast. Somewhere ahead the golden rays of the sunset must be glowing on white beaches and a wide ocean.

The stream at which Mackenzie was gazing came to be known later by the ominous name of the Bad River. It was a tributary of the mighty Fraser River, but a very mean and unpleasant one. No sooner was Mackenzie's poor, long-suffering canoe launched than the fast current of the Bad River began to misuse it. The craft was thrown first onto a sandy bar, then onto a rock that broke some of the ribs, and then onto a great boulder that smashed in the bow. White-foamed water came pouring in over the canoe's crippled sides and the

voyageurs shouted with alarm. One by one they leaped into the water, including Mackenzie and his dog. Downstream they went, swept along by that evil, rock-studded river, while they held onto the canoe and prayed for deliverance from this fresh danger.

A friendly sandbank saved them. They crawled ashore, dragging the ruined canoe behind them. Some of their gear had been washed away, including a quantity of provisions. They were left with sufficient food to last thirty days, one hundred and fifty bullets for their muskets, a fair quantity of bird shot, and a small keg of gunpowder.

"By all the saints, we can go no farther, *monsieur!*" said one of the scared, cold, and drenched *voyageurs*. "We have spoken to this guide of ours. He declares that hostile tribes inhabit the uplands that reach down to the coast. They will certainly murder us if we go among them."

Mackenzie remained utterly determined. Somehow he managed to raise the spirits of those French Canadians and get them to agree to go forward with him once again. Next morning he set them to work building a new canoe.

They went on down the Bad River, risking their lives almost every yard of the way. Instead of being chilled to the bone by day and night, they were now perspiring in the June heat. The mosquitoes, sand flies, and deer flies were driving them frantic, and the river, instead of becoming better the farther down it they went, grew worse every day. All these hardships were too much for the Indian guide. He rose from his sleeping place one night and disappeared. About the same time, Mackenzie's faithful dog, which had accompanied him all the way from Fort Chipewyan, also vanished.

Although left without a guide, Mackenzie remembered the Indian's instructions: "You will come to a river (the Blackwater) that flows in from the west. There you will find an overland trail which leads to the coast. It is one much used by Indians. Follow it, and you will come to the sea—if the tribes do not kill you on the way."

Mackenzie found the river. They unloaded the canoe, stored it in the shade of some trees, and prepared to march the rest of the way. Although Mackenzie himself had some idea of the distance they must travel, none of the other men knew that the coast still lay two hundred and fifty miles away by the most direct route. Both Mackenzie and Mackay carried a seventy-pound load, and each of the sturdy *voyageurs* had a burden weighing one hundred pounds, including a gun and ammunition.

They set off on the last stage of their journey on July 4. The well-worn Indian trail lay through rain-soaked forest, across hilly,

swampy country, and dry, sun-baked valleys. Every now and then they came to lonely little lakes enclosed by soft green hills. A week later they met another tribe of Indians—the most attractive they had ever seen.

The hair of the women was tied in large loose knots over the ears and plaited with great neatness. . . . Some of them had adorned their tresses with beads, with a

> very pretty effect. The men were clothed in leather, their hair was nicely combed, and their complexion was fairer . . . or perhaps they were more clean than any of the natives we had yet seen. Their eyes . . . were of a grey hue with a tinge of red. There was one man amongst them of at least six feet four inches in height . . . he was about twenty-eight years of age and was treated with respect by his party.

On July 16 Mackenzie was trudging up the side of the lofty hills that stood between them and the Bella Coola River, which flows into the Pacific Ocean 100 miles north of Vancouver. Once again packed snowdrifts lay across their path, and sudden squalls lashed the utterly weary men with hail and icy rain. The wind was bitterly cold and numbed their bodies so greatly that when the time came to rest their frozen fingers were

unable to unfasten the straps that held their packs.

They came down at last from those freezing mountains to forests of pine, spruce, elder, and cedar trees, where deer grazed in great numbers. Flowers were blooming, wild fruit was ripening on the trees, and the air was warm and moist. Even the most despondent man in Mackenzie's party realized that they must, indeed, be drawing close to the sea.

The kindness and hospitality of the salmon-fishing Indian tribes who lived along the banks of the rivers was in keeping with their attractive appearance. They lived in villages and their houses, built of cedar, were surprisingly handsome and well-furnished. Mackenzie, accustomed to rough-and-ready meals ever since his childhood, became enthusiastic over the food with which he and his men were served. As fish was the favorite diet of his *voyageurs*, they shared his approval.

The Indians, sturdy men though they were, were astonished at the great loads carried by Mackenzie and his men. "We are grieved to see you traveling in this manner," one said. "Come, let us take you in our canoes."

The *voyageurs*, grinning at the thought of being passengers instead of paddlers for once in a lifetime, took their seats in fine big cedar canoes hollowed out of massive tree trunks. The current was running at a fair six miles an hour, and there were wood and stone fishweirs at frequent intervals, over which the water raced in a mighty white torrent. To the utter horror of the French Canadians, the Indian paddlers steered the canoes straight into these ugly deathtraps and almost literally leaped over the weirs. They managed this extraordinary feat without shipping a drop of water. Safely ashore again, the *voyageurs* were unusually quiet.

"We have been told often enough we are the best canoemen in the world," Ducette confessed to Mackenzie. "Maybe we had come to believe it. Alas, we have seen now that these Indians are greater experts than ourselves! I would not have taken a canoe over those fishweirs for all the rum in Canada!"

At eight o'clock on Saturday morning, July 20, 1793, another larger canoe brought Mackenzie from the mouth of the Bella Coola River into a wide and rocky inlet. It was

a foggy day with a warm, wet westerly wind ruffling the water. Seals, porpoises, gulls, and ducks were everywhere. The air was heavy with the smell of salt water, seaweed, and wet sand. The long journey was ended. Peter Pond's dream of a pathway to the west had come true at last.

Any other explorer might have filled a page or two of his diary with rejoicing remarks. Mackenzie's slow, careful, sober Scots nature prevented him from demonstrating any glee.

> At about eight we got out of the river, which discharges itself by various channels into an arm of the sea. The tide was out and had left a large space covered with seaweed. The surrounding hills were involved in fog.

Perhaps the thought of the limited supplies

that remained in their packs kept Mackenzie from feeling too much pleasure. All they had left were twenty pounds of pemmican, fifteen pounds of rice, and six pounds of flour. Awaiting them was the same long journey back to Fort Chipewyan. If game and fish proved short on the way, they were almost certain to die of starvation. But one thing had to be done before they set off on the homeward trail.

> I now mixed up some vermilion (bright scarlet paint) in melted grease, and inscribed in large characters on the southeast face of the rock on which we had slept, this brief memorial: "Alexander Mackenzie, from Canada by land, the twenty-second of July, 1793."

With these few laconic words Mackenzie placed on record the achievement of his epic

journey. The location of this rock is still known.

For more than two hundred years men like Cartier, Radisson, Champlain, and the great Samuel Hearne had dreamed of making that same overland journey and reaching the far west coast. Through no fault of their own they had failed. Innumerable other men, whose names are unknown to the pages of history, had been even less fortunate. They were the ones who had merely left their bones to whiten by the wayside of the lonely forest trails.

Now that Mackenzie of the Northwest Fur Company had succeeded where all others had failed even the towering barrier of the Rocky Mountains could no longer deter those who would surely follow in his footsteps. First would come the fur traders and trappers, then the prospectors, and finally the settlers. Mackenzie had thrown open the gates to a new westward route. The softer, milder climate of the Pacific shore would soon attract men of all classes from more easterly areas of the American continent. And, as history was soon to disclose, the arrival of those settlers would prevent Russia and Spain from permanently establishing their claim to the Canadian northwest.

However much Mackenzie and his *voyageurs* may have wished to linger on this friendly

coast where food was plentiful, their shortage of the most necessary provisions made such delay impossible. On the morning of July 23 they began the return journey.

Their packs filled with dried salmon, picking edible berries as they went, and with the two Indian hunters ranging ahead all the time in search of game, they trudged up the mountainside. From the pleasant summer heat on the coast they passed into a region of

snow and freezing cold. The last of the salmon was soon eaten, but now they were coming to places where Mackenzie had prudently cached bags of pemmican.

On the fourth of August they reached the end of the overland trail. They found their canoe unharmed where they had left it under the trees. Once again they reached the Parsnip River. Now the current was with them, and the men were growing accustomed to the turbulent, treacherous mountain floods. Fish remained plentiful, and the *voyageurs*, rejoicing and tireless because they were now homeward bound, ate great quantities of whitefish, trout, and carp. Mackenzie's faithful dog, which had been lost for so long, was again with them. The poor half-starved animal had remained beside the trail, waiting for his master to pass that way again.

This time Mackenzie did not attempt to pass through the Peace River Canyon. Instead he portaged around it, another eight or nine weary, backbreaking miles. The late summer weather had brought an abundance of wild game. Day after day the hunters returned to camp, staggering under as much freshly killed meat as they could carry. The Peace River bore them along swiftly and safely to their journey's end.

August 24, 1793: Thus we landed at four

in the afternoon, at the place which we had left on the ninth of May. Here my voyages of discovery terminate. . . . I received, however, the reward of my labours, for they were crowned with success. I have now resumed the character of a trader.

At only thirty years of age Mackenzie had finished with exploration. He was rightly content to have made a dream come true. He had crossed the American continent at its greatest width and thus linked the Atlantic with the Pacific. During the next few years the Northwest Company built a chain of trading posts into the Rockies and opened up trade on the Pacific slopes.

Back in Montreal, shrewd, thrifty Mackenzie made a fortune for himself in the fur trade. He published the story of his travels and was knighted by the English king. In 1808, while still regarded as the greatest of living explorers, he retired to Scotland. Four years later Sir Alexander Mackenzie married a Scottish lady, and eight years later, in the year 1820, he died at the age of fifty-seven.